LEAN AND GREEN DIET RECIPES

Lean and Green Diet Cookbook to Help You to Achieve a Life-long Transformation.

Quick and easy Beginners Guide.

Diamond Connors – DC PRESS

Lean & Green....... *Errore. Il segnalibro non è definito.*

Recipes .... *Errore. Il segnalibro non è definito.*

—

Virginia's Tuna Salad

(Ready in a brief time frame, Serve 2, Difficulty: Easy) Nutrition per Serving: Calories: 121, Proteins: 9.9 g, Carbohydrates: 3.9 g, Fat: 9.8 g, Cholesterol: 59.9mg, Sodium: 167.5mg.

Fixings:

* *1 egg*

* *1(5 ounces) container of fish, exhausted and chipped*

* *3 tablespoons of mayonnaise*

* *2 stems of celery, sliced*

* *2 tablespoons of sweet pickle relish*

* *1 spot of ground dull pepper*

Rules:

1. Put the egg in a dish and cover it with cold water.

2. Heat the water with the eventual result of bubbling and kill it from the hotness right away.

3. Cover the egg and grant it rest for 10-12 minutes in steaming hot water. Wipe out from the warmed water and chill for around 5 minutes. Strip and hack into downsized bits.

4. Mix the fish and mayonnaise in a medium dish. Mix the egg, celery, sauce, and dim pepper.

(Arranged presently, Serve 8, Difficulty: Normal) Nutrition per Serving: Calories: 123, Proteins: 8.2 g, Carbohydrates: 34.6 g, Fat: 7.3 g, Cholesterol: 0mg, Sodium: 222.1mg.

Fixings:

- *1 cup of dry green lentils*

- *2 cups of water*

- *4 tablespoons of isolated olive oil*

- *1 cup of basmati rice*

- *1 colossal of onion, cut*

- *¾ teaspoon salt, or to taste*

Headings:

1. Place the lentils in a dish and cover them with water.

2. Bring to a turning bubble over high hotness for 5 minutes, and afterward, by then, cover and dispense with it from the hotness.

3. Meanwhile, in cool water, wash the rice until the water is perfect.

4. Over medium hotness, heat 2 tablespoons of olive or vegetable oil in a skillet. For around 1 second, rush in the rice until the grains turn cloudy and white, then, add the lentils and water.

5. Pass the rice mix on to a stew, then, cover and lessen the hotness for 5 minutes to medium-low. Blend once, then, cover and further lessening the hotness to a base.

6. Cook, fixed, until the rice is fragile, around 15 extra minutes (don't take out the top!).

7. Meanwhile, over medium hotness, heat the extra 2 tablespoons of oil in the skillet. Blend in the onion, and cook and blend for around 5 minutes until the onion is fragile and clear.

8. Decrease hotness to medium-low and continue cooking and mixing, 15-20 minutes more until the onion is very fragile and dull brown.

8. Blend in the caramelized onion when the rice is ready and season with salt.

(Arranged quickly, Serve 4, Difficulty: Normal) Nutrition per Serving: Calories: 243, Proteins: 9 g, Carbohydrates: 15 g, Fat: 15 g, Saturates: 2 g, Sugars 14 g, Fiber 4 g, Salt 0.3 g.

Fixings:

- *1 immense banana*

- *2 medium eggs, beaten*

- *1 spot of baking powder (without gluten if coeliac)*

- *1 sprinkle of vanilla concentrate*

- *1 teaspoon of oil*

- *25 g of for the most part cut pecans*

- *125 g of raspberries*

Rules:

1. Pound one gigantic banana with a fork in a bowl until it resembles a thick paste.

2. Blend in 2 beaten eggs, a spot of baking powder, and a sprinkle of vanilla concentrate (sans gluten if coeliac).

3. Over medium hotness, heat a colossal non-stick skillet or hotcake dish and shower with 1/2 teaspoon of oil.

4. Spoon 2 hotcakes into the dish with ½ the flour, cook each side for 1-2 minutes, then, tip them onto a plate.

5. With another 1/2 teaspoon of oil and the abundance hitter, reiterate the association.

6. Use the 25 g of by and large hacked pecans and 125 g of raspberries to top the hotcakes.

(Arranged rapidly, Serve 4, Difficulty: Normal) Nutrition per Serving: Calories: 231, Proteins: 8 g, Carbohydrates: 37 g, Fat: 4 g,

Drenches: 1 g, Sugars: 10 g, Fiber: 6 g, Salt: 0.2 g.

Fixings:

* *75 g of quinoa*

* *25 g of porridge oats*

* *4 cardamom cases*

* *250ml of unsweetened almond milk*

* *2 prepared peaches, cut into cuts*

* *1 teaspoon of maple syrup*

Rules:

1. In a shallow pot, combine 250ml of water and 100ml of almond milk to the quinoa, cereal, and cardamom units. Stew carefully, blending regularly, for 15 minutes.

2. Pour in the overabundance almond milk and cook until smooth for an additional 5 minutes.

3. Wipe out the pods of cardamom, spoon them into bowls or pots, then, add the peaches and maple syrup quite far.

Kale, Tomato and Poached Egg on Toast

(Arranged presently, Serve 3, Difficulty: Normal) Nutrition per Serving: Calories: 251, Proteins: 15 g, Carbohydrates: 18 g, Fat: 12 g,

Drenches: 3 g, Sugars: 2 g, Fiber: 3 g, Salt: 0.8 g.

Fixings:

- 2 teaspoon of oil

- 100 g of arranged hacked kale

- 1 clove of garlic, crushed

- ½ teaspoon of stew drops

- 2 immense eggs

- 2 cuts of multigrain bread

• *50 g of divided cherry tomatoes*

• *15 g of crumbled feta*

Headings:

1. Change the hotness so a wide water skillet is warmed with the eventual result of bubbling.

2. Heat the oil over medium-hot hotness in an iron and add the kale, garlic, and stew chips.

3. Cook for 4 minutes, blending reliably until the kale starts to new and withers to 1/2 its size. Set aside.

4. Water rises to a moving air pocket, and the eggs are poached for 2 minutes. Toast the bread.

5. With an opened spoon, kill the poached eggs and cover each cut of toast with half

of the kale, the egg, the cherry tomatoes,
and the feta.

(Arranged rapidly, Serve 6, Difficulty: Normal) Nutrition per Serving: Calories: 215, Proteins: 13 g, Carbohydrates: 54 g, Fat: 6 g, Saturated: 2.8 g, Sodium: 200mg, Sugars: 22 g

Fixings:

• 6 tablespoons of porridge oats

• Essentially under ½ x 200ml tub 0% fat Greek-style yogurt

• ½ x 350 g of pack frozen blueberries

• 1 teaspoon of honey(optional)

Rules:

1. Put the oats with 400 ml of water in a non-stick skillet and cook overheat, rarely blending, until thickened, for around 2 minutes. Wipe out and join 33% of the yogurt from the hotness.

2. Meanwhile, carefully poaching until the blueberries have thawed out and are sensitive, while at this point keeping their construction, tip the blueberries into a skillet with 1 tablespoon of water and the honey.

3. Spoon the porridge into bowls, top the blueberries with the extra yogurt, and spoon over.

Eggy Spelt Bread with Orange Cheese and Raspberries

(Arranged instantly, Serve 2, Difficulty: Normal) Nutrition per Serving: Calories: 197, Proteins: 14 g, Carbohydrates: 12 g, Fat: 10 g, Saturates: 3 g, Sugars: 4 g, Fiber: 2 g, Salt: 0.6 g.

Fixings:

- *2 medium eggs*

- *2 tablespoons of pressed orange*

- *2 cuts of spelt bread, separated*

- *50 g of low-fat curds*

- *1 teaspoon of orange punch*

- *1 teaspoon of rapeseed oil*

- *50 g of raspberries*

- *Clear honey, to serve (optional)*

Rules:

1. In a bowl wide with the eventual result of fitting the bread in it, beat the eggs and crushed orange. Assimilate the bread the eggs and milk for 2 minutes or something to that effect, turning somewhat through.

2. Meanwhile, blend the cheddar and orange punch in a shallow bowl. Put the rapeseed oil over high hotness in a non-stick skillet. Add the eggy bread when warmed.

3. Give to cook flawless for two or three minutes, then, flip and cook for another 1-2 minutes on the contrary side.

3. Parcel the bread into 2 skillet, spot up the cheddar, followed, expecting you like, by the raspberries and honey.

Rich Mustard Mushrooms on Toast with A Glass of Juice

(Ready in a brief time frame, Serve 6, Difficulty: Easy) Nutrition per Serving: Calories: 220, Proteins: 13 g, Carbohydrates: 28 g, Fat: 7 g, Saturates: 2 g, Sugars: 16 g, Fiber: 4 g, Salt: 0.1 g.

Fixings:

- *1 cut of whole meal bread*

- *1 ½ tablespoon of light cheddar cream*

- *1 teaspoon of rapeseed oil*

- *3 small bunches of cut, minimal level mushrooms*

- *2 tablespoons skimmed milk*

- ¼ teaspoon of wholegrain mustard

- 1 tablespoon of cut chives

- 150ml of pressed orange recently squashed or from a holder

Headings:

1. Toast the bread, then, sprinkle (don't use spread) with a little cheddar.

2. Meanwhile, in a non-stick skillet, heat the oil and cook the mushrooms, blending reliably, until they are loose. Spoon in cream, extra cheddar, and mustard.

3. Until covered, blend well. Cover with chives.

4. Present with the juice on the bread.

(Arranged in the blink of an eye, Serve 4, Difficulty: Normal) Nutrition per Serving: Calories: 226, Proteins: 22 g, Carbs: 0 g, Fat: 15 g, Saturates: 5 g, Sugars: 0 g, Fiber: 1 g, Salt 1.1 g.

Fixings:

- *1 teaspoon of oil*

- *80 g of chestnut mushrooms, cut*

- *50 g of diced ham*

- *80 g of sack spinach*

- *4 medium eggs, beaten*

- *1 tablespoon of ground cheddar*

Headings:

1. Heat the grill to its most outrageous setting.

2. Over medium-high pressure, heat the oil in an oven safe skillet. Tip in the mushrooms and fry until generally loose, for 2 minutes.

3. Blend in the ham and spinach, and stew until the spinach has wilted for another 1 min.

4. Season well with dim pepper and a spot of salt.

5. Reduce the hotness and pour the eggs over them. Cook for 3 minutes undisturbed until the eggs are by and large wrapped up.

6. Sprinkle over the cheddar and spot it for 2 minutes under the grill.

Cranberry and Raspberry Smoothie

(Prepared shortly, Serve 6, Difficulty: Easy) Nutrition per Serving: Calories: 100, Proteins: 4 g, Carbohydrates: 17 g, Fat: 2 g, Saturates: 1 g, Sugars: 17 g, Fiber: 1 g, Salt: 0.16 g.

Ingredients:

- 200ml of cranberry juice

- 176 g of frozen thawed out raspberry

- 100ml of milk

- 200ml of regular yogurt

- 1 tablespoon of caster sugar, or to taste

- Mint branches, to serve

Guidelines:

1. In a blender, put every one of the ingredients and interaction until smooth.

2. Fill glasses and serve with new mint covering.

Asparagus Soldiers with a Soft-Boiled Egg

*(Prepared quickly, Serve 6, Difficulty: Easy)
Nutrition per Serving: Calories: 186,
Proteins: 12 g, Carbohydrates: 12 g, Fat:
10 g, Saturates: 2 g, Sugars: 0 g, Fiber: 2
g, Salt: 0.72 g.*

Ingredients:

- *1 tablespoon of olive oil*

- *50 g of fine dry breadcrumbs*

- *1 squeeze every stew and paprika*

- *16-20 asparagus lances*

- *4 eggs*

Directions:

1. In a skillet, heat the oil, add the breadcrumbs, and then, at that point, fry until brilliant and fresh.

2. Season with flavors and flaky ocean salt, then, at that point, pass on to cool.

3. In a huge skillet of bubbling salted water, cook the asparagus until delicate for 3-5 minutes.

4. Heat up the eggs simultaneously for 3-4 minutes.

5. On a plate, put each egg in an egg cup.

6. Channel and split the asparagus between plates.

7. Dissipate and serve over the morsels.

(Prepared in a short time, Serve 6, Difficulty: Normal) Nutrition per Serving: Calories: 179, Proteins: 3 g, Carbohydrates: 31 g, Fat: 6 g, Saturates: 0 g, Sugars: 21 g, Fiber: 4 g, Salt: 0.37 g.

Ingredients:

- *4 ready pears*

- *1 handle of margarine*

- *½ teaspoon of blended zest*

- *2 tablespoons of clear honey*

- *50 g of cornflake*

- *25 g of toasted chipped almond*

Directions:

1. Heat stove to 200 degrees Celsius(392 F)/.

2. Deeply, cut the pears in ½ longwise, then, at that point, top with a small spread handle and a sprinkling of blended flavor.

3. Put the pears in a shallow baking dish, then, at that point, broil for 5 minutes before they begin to relax.

4. In the interim, in a huge microwave bowl, heat the honey and one more handle of spread for 30 sec. Throw the cornflakes and nuts.

5. Remove the pears from the stove and then, at that point, add the cornflake blend to the top. Cook for one more moment or before a dull brilliant shading assumes control over the cornflakes.

6. Permit to cool for a couple of moments, then, at that point, serve warm with frozen yogurt (the cornflakes fresh up again when they cool).

(Prepared shortly, Serve 1, Difficulty: Normal) Nutrition per Serving: Calories: 189, Proteins: 19 g, Carbohydrates: 6 g, Fat: 11 g, Saturates: 4 g, Sugars: 1 g, Fiber: 1 g, Salt: 0.79 g.

Ingredients:

- *225 g of self-rising flour*

- *50 g of plain flour*

- *1 teaspoon of baking powder*

- *½ level teaspoon of bicarbonate of pop*

- *¼ teaspoon of salt*

- *½ level teaspoon of mustard powder*

- *100 g of solid cheddar, half ground and half cubed*

*   *6 tablespoon of vegetable oil*

*   *150 g of Greek yogurt*

*   *125ml of milk*

*   *1 egg*

*   *1 tablespoon of Worcestershire sauce*

Directions:

1. Heat stove to 200 C(392 F)/.

2. In a cup, consolidate oneself raising and plain flour, baking powder, baking pop, salt, and mustard powder.

3. Blend the cheddar, oil, yogurt, and sugar, egg, and Worcestershire sauce in a different bowl.

4. Join every one of the ingredients in the biscuit tin and split between the biscuit cases.

5. Place for 20-25 minutes in the stove until brilliant. On a rack, eliminate and cool somewhat.

6. What you want: request that the youngsters assist with preparing everything, weighing scales, estimation bottle, fork, 2 blending bowls, 12 paper biscuit cases, biscuit box, cheddar grater, sharp blade, cooling rack, and tablespoon.

Hash Browns with Mustard and Smoked Salmon

(Prepared in a short time, Serve 4, Difficulty: Normal) Nutrition per Serving: Calories: 129, Proteins: 9 g, Carbohydrates: 18 g, Fat: 6 g, Saturates: 2 g, Sugars: 1 g, Fiber: 1 g, Salt: 1.61 g.

Ingredients:

- *1 enormous potato (about350 g/12 ounces), washed*

- *1 tablespoon of plain flour*

- *1 tablespoon of wholegrain mustard or horseradish sauce*

- *1 tablespoon of sunflower oil*

- *4 cuts of smoked salmon*

- *1 handle of margarine*

- *To Serve:*

- *Soured cream or crème Fraiche*

- *Chives*

Guidelines:

1. On a clean tea towel, grind the unpeeled potato. Raise the towel edges, and crush over the sink to clean the potatoes off of any abundance water. Place the flour and the mustard or horseradish in a bowl. Season well and join.

2. Partition the combination into 8 circles, then, at that point, with your hands, straighten it.

3. With the margarine and oil, heat an enormous griddle, then, at that point, add the potatoes to the skillet.

4. Cook on each side for 2-3 minutes, over medium hotness, until brilliant.

5. On each serving plate, stack a couple of hash tans and get done with a cut of smoked salmon, a bit of splashed cream or crème Fraiche, and a chives to serve.

(Prepared shortly, Serve 6, Difficulty: Easy) Nutrition per Serving: Calories: 212, Proteins: 2 g, Carbohydrates: 25 g, Fat: 10 g,

Soaks: 0.1 g, Sugars: 24 g, Fiber: 5 g, Salt: 0.01 g.

Ingredients:

- *1 little ready banana*

- *Around 140 g of blackberries, blueberries, raspberries, or strawberries (or utilize a blend)*

- *Squeezed apple or mineral water (Optional)*

- *To Serve:*

- *Runny honey*

*   Blackberries, blueberries, raspberries, or strawberries*

Guidelines:

1. In your blender or food processor, cut the banana and add your preferred berries.

2. Whizz until smooth. Pour in juice or water with the cutting edges buzzing to construct the consistency you want.

3. Throw on top of a couple of extra bananas, shower with honey and berries, then, at that point, serve.

Slow Cooked Corned Beef for Sandwiches

(Ready in 4 hours and 15 minutes, Serve 1, and Difficulty: Normal) Nutrition per Serving: Calories: 229, Proteins: 15 g, Carbohydrates: 4.2 g, Fat: 15.1 g, Cholesterol: 77.9 mg, Sodium: 904.3 mg.

Fixings:

- *2(1360 g) of corned cheeseburger briskets with flavor groups*

- *2(12 fluid ounces) containers of blend*

- *2 inlet leaves*

- *¼ cup of peppercorns*

- *1 bulb of clove garlic, secluded and stripped*

Rules:

1. Place the briskets with the corned burger in an immense pot. Sprinkle with 1 of the packages of flavor and discard the other or save it for various purposes. Pour in the blend and fill the pot with adequate water to cover 1 inch of the briskets. Add the sound leaves, garlic, and peppercorns.

2. Decline the hotness to medium-low until the liquid arrives at edge of boiling over, then, stew for 4-5 hours, checking hourly and adding more water if important to keep the meat covered.

3. Dispense with the meat from the pot steadily, as it will be irrefutably fragile. Set it on a cutting board and grant it to rest for around 10 minutes before it firms up a little.

4. To serve, cut or shred, discard the cooking liquid, yet it will in general be used for cooking cabbage and various vegetables at whatever point needed.

(Arranged rapidly, Serve 4, Difficulty: Normal) Nutrition per Serving: Calories: 210, Proteins: 8.9 g, Carbohydrates: 34.6 g, Fat: 4.3 g, Cholesterol: 0 mg, Sodium: 997.3 mg.

Fixings:

- *Olive oil*

- *1 huge onion, diced*

- *2 cloves of garlic, or more to taste*

- *2 cups of pureed tomatoes*

- *24 ounces of arranged cannellini beans*

- *1 tablespoon of dried basil*

- *½ teaspoon of oregano*

- *Salt and ground dim pepper, to taste*

Rules:

1. over medium heat the olive oil to high hotness in a pot. In hot oil, cook and blend onion until sensitive, around 5 minutes, add garlic and keep on cooking until fragrant, around 1-2 extra minutes.

2. Add the pureed tomatoes to the pot and blend. Add the peppers, basil, oregano, salt, and pepper to the cannellini.

3. Heat the blend with the eventual result of bubbling, decline the hotness to medium-low, and cook 5-7 extra minutes until the beans are hot.

Zesty Grilled Cheese Sandwich

(Ready in a brief time frame, Serve 6, Difficulty: Easy) Nutrition per Serving: Calories: 213, Proteins: 10.7 g, Carbohydrates: 28.2 g, Fat: 22.1 g, Cholesterol: 57.2 mg, Sodium: 846.4 mg.

Fixings:

- *2 tablespoons of spread or margarine*

- *4 cuts of white bread*

- *2 cuts of American cheddar*

- *1 roman (plum) tomato, pitifully cut*

- *¼ little onion, cut*

- *1 jalapeno pepper, cut*

Rules:

1. Over low hotness, heat a colossal skillet. Spread or margarine north of 2 cuts of bread on 1 side.

2. Place the buttered side of the two pieces in the skillet. Place each one with a cut of cheddar and top with the tomato, onion, and jalapeno strips.

3. Spread the extra cuts of bread on one side and put them on top of the buttered side. In the event that the sandwiches are toasted at the base, flip and fry until the contrary side is brown.

(Ready in 1 hour and 25 minutes, Serve 4, Difficulty: Hard) Nutrition per Serving: Calories: 306, Proteins: 25.3 g, Carbohydrates: 15.7 g, Fat: 15.7 g, Cholesterol: 78.7 mg, Sodium: 1398.8 mg.

Fixings:

• 680 g of boneless meat throw, cut into 2-inch pieces

• Salt and ground dim pepper, to taste

• 1 tablespoon of vegetable oil

• 6 cloves of garlic, cut

• 2 tablespoons of white vinegar

• 1 tablespoon of dried oregano

- *1 ½ teaspoon of salt, or to taste*

- *1 teaspoon of dried thyme*

- *1 teaspoon of dried rosemary*

- *1 teaspoon of recently ground dull pepper*

- *1 straight leaf*

- *¼ teaspoon of red pepper pieces, or to taste*

- *3 cups of chicken stock, or dependent upon the situation*

- *4 dry bread rolls, cut in ½*

- *1 cup of cut giardiniera (relieved Italian vegetables)*

- *2 teaspoons of cut new level leaf parsley*

Headings:

1. Season the meat with a spot of dim pepper and salt. Heat the vegetable oil over high hotness in a significant pot. Cook and blend the meat until sautéed in hot oil, for 5-8 minutes.

2. Poon the meat with dim pepper, straight leaf, and red pepper drops. Void adequate chicken stock into the cheeseburger mix to cover 1 inch of the meat and convey it to a stew.

3. Cover the pot with a top, decline the hotness to low, and stew for 1-1 1/2 hour until the meat is fork fragile.

4. Move meat to an alternate pot with a sifter or opened spoon and pour around 1/4 cup of meat stock into the pot. To carefully break the meat into more unobtrusive pieces, use a wooden spoon. Use a top or aluminum foil to cover the pot and keep it warm.

5. Season with salt and pepper to taste. Skim the excess oil from the most elevated mark of the stock extra in the fundamental pot. Use a top or aluminum foil to cover the pot and keep the stock warm.

6. On a work surface, lay the pieces of a rollout and spoon 2-3 tablespoons of meat stock over each 1/2. A liberal piece of meat and a spoonful of restored vegetables are on top of the roll's base ½. Put the top on the sandwich.

7. Repeat to make three more sandwiches with the extra buns, stock, meat, and relieved vegetables.

8. Spoon the hot meat stock into ramekins and top 1/2 teaspoon of parsley with each ramekin. For plunging, serve sandwiches with hot stock.

(Ready in 8 hours and 10 minutes, Serve 1, Difficulty: Hard) Nutrition per Serving: Calories: 318, Proteins: 39.4 g, Carbohydrates: 1.6 g, Fat: 15.8 g, Cholesterol 100.4 mg, Sodium: 819.1 mg.

Fixings:

- *1(3721 g) back supper*

- *3 cups of water*

- *2 tablespoons of dried basil*

- *1 tablespoon of dried oregano*

- *1 tablespoon of salt*

- *1 tablespoon of garlic powder*

- *1 tablespoon of parsley drops*

- *3 river leaves*

- *1 ½ teaspoons of red pepper drops*

- *⅓ teaspoon of ground dull pepper, or to taste*

Rules:

1. In a drowsy cooker, join the dish, basil, water, oregano, cinnamon, garlic powder, red pepper pieces, parsley drops, bay leaves, and dull pepper.

2. In a drowsy cooker, cook for 8-10 hours, set to low. Use 2 forks to kill limits leaves and shred meat

Sustenance per Serving: Calories: 199, Proteins: 14.1 g, Carbohydrates: 30.2 g, Fat: 2.9 g, Cholesterol 9.6 mg, Sodium: 341.4 mg. (Ready in 6 hours and 30 minutes, Serve 10, Difficulty: Hard)

Fixings:

• 6 cups of water

• 1 3D square of chicken bouillon

• 453 g of organized, washed and, dried dull checked peas out

• 1 onion, diced

• 2 cloves of garlic, diced

• 1 red ringer pepper, stemmed, developed, and diced

- *1 jalapeno chile, developed and minced*

- *8 ounces of diced ham*

- *4 cuts of bacon, hacked*

- *½ teaspoon of cayenne pepper*

- *1 ½ teaspoon of cumin*

- *Salt, to taste*

- *1 teaspoon of ground dull pepper*

Bearings:

1. Void the water into a drowsy cooker to separate, add the bouillon strong shape, and blend.

2. Mix in obscurity looked toward peas, the onion, the jalapeno pepper, the garlic, the toll pepper, the ham, the cayenne pepper, the bacon, the salt, and the pepper, and mix well. Cover the drowsy cooker and stew for 6-8 hours, until the beans are fragile.

Mother's Sushi Rice

(Ready in 1 hour and 5 minutes, Serve 10, Difficulty: Hard) Nutrition per Serving: Calories: 318, Proteins: 2.9 g, Carbohydrates: 40.7 g, Fat: 0.2 g, Cholesterol 0 mg, Sodium: 296.2 mg.

Fixings:

- *2 ¼ cups of Japanese sushi-style rice*

- *1(4 inch) piece of kombu dried kelp*

- *3 cups of water*

- *¼ cup of rice vinegar*

- *¼ cup of white sugar*

- *1 ¼ teaspoon of salt*

Rules:

1. Put the rice in a significant, gigantic bowl. Cover the rice with cold water and rub it with your hands until the water turns smooth white. Spill the obscure water out, taking thought not to spill the rice out. Go over 3 or multiple times before the rice ought to be apparent through 3 drags of water.

2. Divert the rice in a fine sifter, then, join it with kombu and 3 cups of water in a pot. Grant it to represent 30 minutes. Combine as one the rice vinegar, sugar, and salt until set aside and split up in a little bowl.

3. Cover and over high hotness, heat rice with the eventual result of bubbling, then, decrease hotness to low and stew for 15 minutes. Dispose of from the hotness and license to represent 5 minutes, covered.

4. In a bowl, scratch the rice, kill, and discard the kombu. Blend in the mix of vinegar until especially united, and no rice bulges remain. License cooling at room temperature. Use an electric fan to quickly cool the rice for a shinier appearance.

(Ready in 1 hour and 10 minutes, Serve 6, Difficulty: Hard) Nutrition per Serving: Calories: 210, Proteins: 3.4 g, Carbohydrates: 19.7 g, Fat: 2.8 g

Fixings:

• 6 ears of recently shucked corn

• 1 green pepper, diced

• 2 Roman(plum) tomatoes, diced

• ¼ cup of diced red onion

• ½ heap of new cilantro, sliced, or to taste

• 2 teaspoons of olive oil, or to taste

• Salt and ground dim pepper, to taste

Bearings:

1. Preheat the medium-hot external grill and carefully oil the grill.

2. On the preheated grill, cook the corn, inconsistently turning, until the corn is sensitive and dull spots appear, set aside for around 10 minutes, until adequately cool to deal with. Remove the parts the cob, then, place them in a bowl.

3. Combine the green pepper, cilantro, diced tomato, onion, and olive oil with the warm corn pieces. , mix until mixed after seasoning with pepper and salt similarly. To allow flavors to blend before serving, set aside for something like 30 minutes.

Measuring utensil's Vegetable Barley Soup

(Ready in 1.5 hours, Serve 8, Difficulty: Hard) Nutrition per Serving: Calories: 188, Proteins: 6.9 g, Carbohydrates: 37 g, Fat: 1.6 g, Cholesterol 0 mg, Sodium: 968.8 mg.

Fixings:

- *2 quarts of vegetable stock*

- *1 cup of uncooked grain*

- *2 tremendous carrots, cut*

- *2 stems of celery, cut*

- *1(14.5 ounces) container of diced tomatoes with juice*

- *1 zucchini, cut*

- *1(15 ounces) container of garbanzo beans, exhausted*

- *1 onion, cut*

- *3 bay leaves*

- *1 teaspoon of garlic powder*

- *1 teaspoon of white sugar*

- *1 teaspoon of salt*

- *½ teaspoon of ground dim pepper*

- *1 teaspoon of dried parsley*

- *1 teaspoon of curry powder*

- *1 teaspoon of paprika*

- *1 teaspoon of Worcestershire sauce*

Headings:

1. In an enormous pot, void the vegetable stock into it. Add the grain, celery, carrots, tomatoes, zucchini, onion, garbanzo beans, and sound leaves.

2. Similarly add to the blend the garlic powder, sugar, curry powder, paprika, salt, pepper, parsley, and Worcestershire sauce. Heat it with the end result of bubbling, then, cover and stew for 90 minutes over medium-low hotness. It'll be very thick with the soup. At whatever point needed, add more stock or less grain.

3. Preceding serving, dispense with the straight leaves.

(Ready in a brief time frame, Serve 4, Difficulty: Normal) Nutrition per Serving Calories: 191, Proteins: 19 g, Carbohydrates: 4 g, Fat: 3 g, Fiber: 0 g, Sugars: 1 g, Sodium: 273 mg.

Fixings:

* *2 tremendous green peppers, split the long way, and developed*

* *453 g of lean ground turkey*

* *1 tablespoon of less sodium taco getting ready*

* *¼ cup of pureed tomatoes*

* *¼ cup of diminished fat sharp cheddar annihilated cheddar*

Rules:

1. Preheat the oven to 176 degree Celsius (350 degrees Fahrenheit).

2. Natural shaded ground turkey in a significant, medium-hot skillet.

3. Add 1 tablespoon of water and the turkey getting ready and blend.

Add the sauce. Add some extra of the meat it is unnecessarily dry to accept it. Exactly when the turkey is warmed totally, turn the hotness to medium.

4. Add cheddar and blend totally.

5. Cut the green peppers, completely into two halves. Cut a semi-circle around the stem, and in one cut, eliminate the stem and seeds.

6. Go over until there are 4 sections.

7. Place the 2 sections in gurgling water for 5 minutes at the same time. Resulting to cooking, the "skin" will lose a little splendor.

8. Place peppers open side up in a baking dish and burden up with your meat blend.

9. Heat for 20-25 minutes in the oven.

10. Spot and sprinkle with your favored trimmings on plates.

Chicago-Inspired Italian Beef Sandwich

(Ready in 1 hour and 25 minutes, Serve 4, Difficulty: Hard) Nutrition per Serving: Calories: 406, Proteins: 29.3 g, Carbohydrates: 35.7 g, Fat: 15.7 g, Cholesterol 78.7 mg, Sodium: 1398.8 mg.

Fixings:

- *1 tablespoon of vegetable oil*

- *6 cloves of garlic, cut*

- *2 tablespoons of white vinegar*

- *1 tablespoon of dried oregano*

- *1 ½ teaspoon of salt, or to taste*

- *1 teaspoon of dried thyme*

- *1 teaspoon of dried rosemary*

- *1 teaspoon of recently ground dim pepper*

- *1 sound leaf*

- *¼ teaspoon of red pepper chips, or to taste*

- *3 cups of chicken stock, or dependent upon the situation*

- *4 dried up bread rolls, cut in ½*

- *1 cup of hacked giardiniera (salted Italian vegetables)*

- *2 teaspoons of hacked new level leaf parsley*

Bearings:

1. With a bit of dull pepper and salt, season the cheeseburger. Heat the vegetable oil in a significant pot over high hotness. Cook and blend the meat for 5-8 minutes before it is sautéed in hot oil.

2. Garlic, vinegar, oregano, 1 1/2 teaspoons of garlic, thyme, rosemary, one teaspoon dull pepper, sound leaf and red pepper are added to the meat. To cover 1 inch of the steak, add adequate chicken stock into the meat mix and convey it to a stew.

3. Use a top to cover the pot, decline the hotness to low.

4. Using a sifter or opened spoon to move meat to another compartment and pour about ½ a cup of meat stock into the pot. Also, use a wooden spoon to gently hole the meat into more unobtrusive pieces. Cover the pot and keep it warm with a cap or aluminum foil.

5. To taste, season with salt and pepper. From the most noteworthy place of the stock left in the essential shower, skim off the extra oil. To keep the stock warm, use a top or aluminum foil to cover the pot.

6. Put the pieces of a rollout on a work surface and spoon 2-3 teaspoons of meat stock over each half. On top of the roll's

lower half is a liberal measure of cheeseburger and a spoonful of salted vegetables. Put on them with sandwich tops. Repeat with the extra buns, soup, meat, and relieved vegetables to make three more sandwiches.

7. Spoon the hot meat stock into ramekins and finish each ramekin with 1/2 teaspoon of parsley. Present with hot stock sandwiches.

(Ready in 6 hours and 20 minutes, Serve 16, and Difficulty: Hard) Nutrition per Serving: Calories: 213, Proteins: 0.5 g, Carbohydrates: 4 g, Fat: 0.9 g, Cholesterol 0 mg, Sodium: 27.5 mg.

Fixings:

• *1 tablespoon of olive oil*

• *2 rotisserie chicken remaining parts, broken into pieces*

• *4 carrots, cut into bumps*

• *2 huge onions, cut into protuberances*

• *3 stems of celery, with leaves*

• *½ cup of dry white wine*

• *1 tablespoon of whole peppercorns*

• *5 whole cloves of garlic*

• *2 river leaves*

• *1 branch new thyme*

• *5 quarts of water*

Rules:

1. Preheat the grill to 400 degrees Fahrenheit (200 degrees Celsius).

2. Top with chicken cadaver pieces, cabbage, onions, and celery. Add olive oil into the lower part of a tremendous cooking holder.

3. Cook in a preheated oven until bones and vegetables are sautéed, mixing regularly for around an hour.

4. Move to a 8-quart stockpot of cooked chicken bones and vegetables. Void the wine into the cooking holder, scour the sides, fill the stockpot to convey any carmelized slices of bread.

5. Fill the stockpot with peppercorns, garlic, limits leaves, and thyme. Cover the blend with water and let it bubble bit by bit. Set the hotness to low and stew for something like 5 hours, pushing off the fat contingent upon the circumstance.

6. Strain stock, refrigerate or freeze stock using a cheesecloth.

(Ready in 3 hours and 20 minutes, Serve 8, and Difficulty: Hard) Nutrition per Serving: Calories: 127, Proteins: 0 g, Carbohydrates: 18.7 g, Fat: 0 g, Cholesterol: 0 mg, Sodium: 41.3 mg.

Fixings:

* *1 bit of baking pop*

* *2 cups of foaming water*

* *6 tea sacks*

* *¾ cup of white sugar*

* *6 cups of cool water*

Rules:

1. In a 64-ounce heat-confirmation glass pitcher, sprinkle a dash of baking pop. Pour in the gurgling water, and afterward, by then, add the tea sacks. Cover, and think about 15 minutes to drench.

2. Wipe out the tea sacks, discard them and race in the sugar until separated.

3. Use cool water to pour in and refrigerate until cold.

Katie's Yogurt Veggie Salad

(Ready in 1 hour and 50 minutes, Serve 4, Difficulty: Hard) Nutrition per Serving: Calories: 311, Proteins: 8.9 g, Carbohydrates: 22 g, Fat: 0.4 g, Cholesterol 3.9 mg, Sodium: 128.9 mg.

Fixings:

• *25 ounces of non-fat plain yogurt*

• *½ colossal English cucumber, separated, developed, and ground*

• *1 carrot, ground*

• *Salt, to taste*

• *½ onion, diced*

• *½ red ringer pepper, diced*

- *1 stem of celery, diced*

- *¼ cup of cut new parsley*

- *¼ lemon, crushed*

- *1 tablespoon of cut new mint, or to taste*

- *2 teaspoons of ground cumin*

- *Salt and ground dim pepper, to taste*

Rules:

1. Spoon the yogurt into a colander fixed with cheesecloth and set it to the side for something like 30 minutes until most of the water has exhausted.

2. Sprinkle with salt and put the ground cucumber and ground carrot in a cheesecloth-lined colander. To drain overflow water, place a significant thing, similar to a bowl, on top of the cucumber and carrot, for 15-20 minutes.

3. In a bowl, mix the milk, cucumber, carrot, cabbage, red toll pepper, celery, parsley, lemon crush, mint, and season with dim salt pepper.

4. Refrigerate for something like 1 hour for the flavors to blend.

(Arranged rapidly, Serve 6, Difficulty: Normal) Nutrition per Serving: Calories: 450, Proteins: 1 g, Carbohydrate: 30 g, Fat: 0 g, Sodium: 0 mg, Sugars: 19 g.

Fixings:

For Banana Idli:

- *1 cup of idli player*

- *4 tablespoons of. jaggery powder*

- *1 spot of salt*

- *1 spot of cardamom powder*

- *½ prepared banana, sliced*

For Coconut Jaggery Cream:

- *1 cup of coconut milk*

- *2 tablespoons of jaggery powder*

Rules:

1. For banana idli, add all of the fixings together.

2. Oil with sugar, spoon some hitter into the structure, and steam until done. When finished, kill it from the shape.

3. Heat the coconut milk in the jaggery sauce and add the jaggery powder. Blend until separated. With warm coconut sauce, serve warm idlis.

(Ready in 4 hours 50 minutes, Serve 6, Difficulty: Hard) Nutrition per Serving: Calories: 132, Proteins: 14 g, Carbohydrates: 51 g, Fat: 11 g, Saturated Fat: 1 g, Fiber: 19 g, Sodium: 535 mg.

Fixings:

- *2 tablespoon of extra virgin olive oil*

- *2 medium carrots, severed*

- *2 stems of celery, cut*

- *medium onion, finely cut*

- *¼ cup of tomato stick*

- *3 cloves of garlic, crushed with press*

- *½ teaspoon of ground cumin*

* *1 teaspoon of smoked paprika*

* *cups of lower-sodium vegetable or chicken stock*

* *containers (15 oz. each one) of lower-sodium dull beans, undrained*

* *1 cup of frozen corn*

For Serving:

* *Avocado pieces and cilantro leaves*

Bearings:

1. In a 12-inch skillet, heat oil on medium-high. Add the carrots, onion, and celery. Cook for 6-8 minutes or until the sautéing begins, blending inconsistently.

2. Add the tomato paste, garlic, and paprika, all smoked. Cook, mixing, until the garlic is splendid and the tomato stick is sautéed, or 1-2 minutes. Blend in an enormous part of a cup of stock and scratch off any natural hued bits.

3. Skillet substance are moved to the 6-8-quart slow-cooker bowl and beans, maize, and staying stock. Using avocado and cilantro to serve.

4. Second Pot Instructions: As shown in the movement, select the cooking part and cook vegetables. Add beans, maize, and stock, then. Select the lazy cooking limit and cook for 4 hours on high or 6 hours on low.

Salmon with Grilled Eggplant and Chickpea Croutons

(Ready in 1 hour and 15 minutes, Serve 4, Difficulty: Normal)

Nutrition per Serving: Calories: 330, Proteins: 37 g, Carbohydrates: 29 g, Fat: 19 g, Saturated Fat: 3.5 g, Sodium: 400 mg, Fiber: 9 g.

Fixings:

* *3 tablespoons notwithstanding 1 teaspoon of olive oil, apportioned*

* *little onion, finely divided*

* *cloves of garlic, crushed, apportioned*

* *Certified salt*

* *1 cup of chickpea flour*

- *1 tablespoon of lemon punch notwithstanding 2 teaspoons of lemon juice*

- *medium eggplants (around 12 ounces each)*

- *567 grams of skinless salmon filet, cut into 4 pieces*

- *¼ cup of plain full-fat yogurt*

- *1 cup of mint leaves, torn*

- *2 tablespoons of divided chives*

Rules:

1. Line 4 1/2 with a 8 1/2-inch material piece holder, leaving the shade on 2 long sides. In a medium skillet heat with 1 tablespoon.

2. Add the onion, ½ the garlic, and ¼ teaspoon of salt, and cook until fragile, from time to time blending, for 5 minutes. Blend in 2 cups of water and hotness it with the end result of bubbling. Bit by bit stream in the chickpea flour while whisking and whisk excitedly, off the hotness, until generally knock free.

3. Move the mix with the lemon punch and puree to the food processor, constantly adding one tablespoon of oil until thoroughly smooth. Move immediately to the pre-arranged smooth top and dish. Cover and push with something profound with another sheet of material and another piece holder. Refrigerate until it is solid.

4. In the meantime, heat a medium-high grill. Break the blend of chickpeas into 1/2-inch strong shapes. In a little skillet, heat 1 teaspoon of oil and cook for 2-3 gatherings, here and there turning, until burned, 3-5 minutes. Move to the paper towel to exhaust.

5. Cut the eggplants 1/2 inch thick longwise. Brush the extra tablespoon of oil with the eggplant cuts, season with a spot of salt, and grill until sensitive and tenderly singed, 3-4 minutes. Season salmon with ¼ teaspoon of salt and pepper each, add to grill close by eggplant, and grill 3-5 minutes for every side until cloudy all through. Moving to plates.

6. Whisk together the yogurt, lemon juice, remaining garlic, and a spot of salt in a little bowl. Give the eggplant the yogurt sauce and sprinkle with the chickpea bread enhancements, mint, and chives.

7. Present with grilled salmon.

(Arranged rapidly, Serve 6, Difficulty: Normal) Nutrition per Serving: Calories: 237, Proteins: 43 g, Carbohydrate: 53 g, Fat: 9.5 g, Saturated Fat: 1.5 g, Sodium: 425 mg, Fiber: 5 g.

Fixings:

• 453 grams of boneless, skinless chicken chests, cut into 1 ½-in pieces

• 1 tablespoon of olive oil

• 1 teaspoon of dried oregano

• 1 teaspoon of ground sumac

• Fit salt and pepper

• 1 16 ounces of grape or cherry tomatoes

• 1 medium onion, by and large cut

• 1 cup of couscous

* *1 teaspoon of ground lemon punch notwithstanding*

* *1 tablespoon of lemon juice*

* *¼ cup of new dill, isolated*

For Serving:

* *Deteriorated feta*

* *Lemon wedges*

Headings:

1. Toss the chicken with the oil in a colossal bowl, then, add the oregano, sumac, and ½ teaspoon of salt and pepper. Add the onion and tomatoes and toss to mix.

2. Organize an even layer in the air fryer holder and fry at 400 degrees Fahrenheit (204 Celsius), shaking the bushel now and again, 15-20 minutes, until chicken is splendid brown and cooked through.

3. In the interim, toss couscous with lemon punch and set up the bearings per box. Fork and cross-over the puff with lemon juice and 2 teaspoons of dill.

4. Serve over couscous chicken and vegetables, spooning over the most elevated mark of any juices accumulated at the lower part of the air fryer. At whatever point needed, sprinkle with the extra dill and feta and present with lemon wedges.

Sautéed Chicken with Lemony Roasted Broccoli

(Ready in a brief time frame, Serve 6, Difficulty: Easy) Nutrition per Serving: Calories: 316, Proteins: 44 g, Carbohydrates: 15 g, Fat: 15.5 g, Saturated Fat: 2.5 g, Sodium: 375 mg, Fiber: 5 g.

Fixings:

- *680 grams of broccoli, cut into florets*

- *2 cloves of garlic, pitifully cut*

- *3 tablespoon of olive oil*

- *Veritable salt and pepper*

- *4 6-ounces of skinless-boneless chicken chest*

o 1 cup of generally helpful flour

• 1 lemon, cut into ½-inch pieces

o 2 tablespoon of lemon juice

Bearings:

1. 425 degrees Fahrenheit (218 degree Celsius) heat in the oven. Toss the broccoli and garlic with 1 tablespoon of oil on the rimmed baking sheet. Cook for 10 minutes and add 1/4 teaspoon of salt and pepper each.

2. In the meantime, season with 1/4 teaspoon of salt and pepper, chicken chests to even thickness, then, coat in flour. Heat 1 tablespoon of oil in a colossal skillet over medium-high hotness and cook 3-5 minutes for each side of chicken until splendid brown. Settle chicken in the point of convergence of broccoli and feast for around 6 minutes until chicken is cooked through and broccoli is splendid brown and fragile.

3. Return the skillet to medium hotness, add the abundance tablespoons of oil, then, the lemon pieces, and cook for 3 minutes, mixing, until splendid. Add lemon juice and 1/3 cup water and cook any carmelized pieces, blending and scratching. Spoon and present with broccoli over chicken.

4. Plan and store the broccoli and lemons for up to 2 days before cooking.

(Ready in a brief time frame, Serve 4, Difficulty: Easy) Nutrition per Serving: Calories: 312, Proteins: 29 g, Carbohydrates: 9 g, Fat: 18 g, Sodium: 735 mg, Fiber: 3 g.

Fixings:

• 1(2" thick) of boneless top flank beefsteak (453 grams)

o 1 tablespoon of vegetable oil

• ½ heap of green onions, separated

• ¾ teaspoon of flaky sea salt

• 1 ½ ounce of holder mixed greens

• ½ little head radicchio, leaves separated and torn

• *4 cooked beets, quartered*

• *¼ cup of red-wine vinegar*

• *1 tablespoon of extra virgin olive oil*

o *2 ounces of blue cheddar, crumbled.*

Headings:

1. Set up the sous vide unit in the 8-quart saucepot as the group facilitates. Add water and set the contraption's temperature to 130 degrees Celsius (266 degrees F).

2. Place the steak in a reseal able plastic pack of a gallon size, seal solidly, push out overflow air. Place your sack in steaming hot water. Cook for 2 hours. Take out the sack from the water. Eliminate the steak from the sack and wipe it off.

3. Heat oil to medium-high until incredibly hot in a 10-inch skillet. Add the green onions and cook for 2 minutes or until delicately consumed. Add steak to skillet. Cook 2 minutes, turning as frequently as could really be expected. Move to a cutting board, sprinkle with ½ teaspoon flaky sea salt, and thickly cut.

4. Toss the greens, radicchio, olive oil, beets, vinegar, and 1/4 teaspoon all of the flaky sea salt and pepper into a gigantic cup. Move to a plate. Place the steak, onions, and blue cheddar on top.

(Arranged in the blink of an eye, Serve 6, Difficulty: Easy) Nutrition per Serving: Calories: 200, Proteins: 29 g, Carbohydrate: 7 g, Fat: 5 g, Saturated Fat: 1 g, Sodium: 905 mg.

Fixings:

o 1 tablespoon notwithstanding 1 teaspoon of low-sodium soy sauce

• 1 tablespoon notwithstanding 1 teaspoon of toasted sesame oil

• ¼ sweet onion, gently cut

o 3 scallions, gently cut

• Genuine salt

• 453 grams of new sushi-grade ahi fish, cut into 1-inch 3D squares

• 1 Persian cucumber, gently cut

• 1 tablespoon of rice vinegar

• ¼ teaspoon of sugar

• 1 teaspoon of dull sesame seeds, as well as something different for sprinkling

• 1 prepared avocado, quartered

For Serving:

• Cooked rice

Bearings:

1. Combine the soy sauce, onion, sesame oil, scallions, and a dash of salt in a huge bowl. Toss and refrigerate with fish until ready for use.

2. Toss the cucumbers with sugar, vinegar, sesame seeds, and a bit of salt in a little cup. Permit the 5 minutes to stand.

3. Right when required, marinated cucumbers, serve fish and avocado over rice. In the event that fundamental, sprinkle with extra dim sesame seeds.

Provincial Smoky Glazed Chicken and Veggie Bake

(Prepared quickly, Serve 6, Difficulty: Easy) Nutrition per Serving: Calories: 270, Proteins: 18 g, Carbohydrate: 23 g, Total Fat: 13 g, Saturated Fat: 3 g, Sodium: 440 mg.

Ingredients:

- *2 teaspoons of smoked paprika*

- *2 teaspoons of ground cumin*

- *½ teaspoon of pepper*

- *Extra-virgin olive oil*

- *Fit salt*

- *453 gramsof potatoes*

- *½ pound of carrots*

- *113 grams of Brussels sprouts*

- *113 grams of onion*

For Serving:

- *Lemon wedges*

Instructions:

1. Preheat the oven to 450 degrees Fahrenheit (232 Celsius). Combine the paprika, and pepper.

2. Combine 2 tablespoons of olive oil, 1/3 rub, and 1/2 teaspoon of salt with potatoes, Brussels sprouts, carrots, and onion on a large rimmed baking sheet. Roast for 10 min.

3. Toss 2 teaspoons of olive oil and one-third of the asparagus, mushrooms, and green beans into another baking dish. Push the pan to one side. Arrange the chicken bits on the other hand. Sprinkle with the rub that remains.

4. Season the Protein and veggies with 1/2 teaspoon of salt. Roast both pans for 20-35 minutes or until all vegetables are softened, and the chicken is cooked (transfer chicken from pan to platter if cooked before veggies are tender). Garnish it with parsley and a squeeze of lemon to serve.

(Arranged in no time, Serve 4, Difficulty: Easy) Nutrition per serving: Calories: 224, Proteins: 14 g, Carbohydrates: 66 g, Fat: 15 g, Saturated Fat: 5 g, Sodium: 510 mg, Fiber: 6 g.

Fixings:

* *Seared vegetables from mustard covered pork severs*

* *4 cup of low-sodium chicken stock*

* *453 grams of thawed out frozen corn*

* *¼ cup of profound cream*

* *2 tablespoon of new lemon juice*

* *½ teaspoon of salt*

* *½ teaspoon of pepper*

* *Broken down bacon and gently cut scallions, at whatever point needed*

Headings:

1. Thyme from held cooked vegetables is discarded, and ½ of them are moved to a gigantic pot. Low-sodium chicken stock should be added and warmed with the end result of bubbling. Smash until smooth, using an immersion blender (or standard blender).

2. Add to the pot the frozen maize (thawed out) and remaining seared vegetables and bring to a stew. Blend in new lemon juice, profound cream, salt, and pepper. At whatever point needed, serve polished off with broke down bacon and gently cut scallions.

(Ready in a brief time frame, Serve 6, Difficulty: Easy) Nutrition per serving: Calories: 230, Proteins: 28 g, Carbohydrates: 11 g, Fat: 16 g Saturated 4.5 g, Sodium: 345 mg, Fiber: 2 g.

Fixings:

* *One 1360 g-1587 g of chicken, including neck (discard giblets), skin disposed of*

* *2 gigantic carrots, split*

o *1 onion, quartered*

* *1 clove of garlic, squashed*

* *1 river leaf*

* *4 parts of parsley*

• *Real salt*

• *1 ½ cup of egg noodles*

For Serving:

• *Separated dill*

• *2 stems of celery, separated, notwithstanding celery leaves*

Rules:

1. Put the chicken in the electric strain cooker, add the carrots, celery, inlet leaf, onion, garlic, parsley, 3/4 teaspoon of salt, and 6 cups of water. Lock and cook for 15 minutes at high strain (12.0). To mitigate pressure, use the quick conveyance process, then, open the cover. Move the chicken to the tub, then, the carrots and celery to the cutting board, and let it cool.

2. Through a fine-network sifter, strain stock in a pot, discard any overabundance solids, move back to the pot, press Cook and pass the mix on to a stew. Add the noodles and cook for 5-6 minutes, until sensitive. Then, press drop.

3. Carrots and celery, in the meantime, are cut into little pieces, and chicken is annihilated into colossal pieces, discarding skin and bones. Blend in the stock and serve, if important, soup sprinkled with dill and celery leaves.

(Arranged in a matter of seconds, Serve 6, Difficulty: Easy) Nutrition per Serving: Calories: 326, Proteins: 6 g, Carbohydrates: 68 g, Fat: 17 g, Saturated Fat: 5 g, Sodium: 510 mg, Fiber: 4 g.

Fixings:

- *12 ounces of mezze rigatoni*

o *1 tablespoon of olive oil*

o *2 cloves of garlic, pressed*

- *453 gramsof ground chicken*

- *½ teaspoon of red pepper pieces*

- *Real salt and pepper*

- *½ cup of dry white wine*

- *½ cup of low-sodium chicken stock*

• *1 tablespoon of finely ground lemon punch*

• *½ cup of finely ground Parmesan cheddar*

• *¾ cup of separated level leaf parsley*

• *1 tablespoon of severed tarragon*

• *¼ cup of separated chives*

o *2 tablespoon of cold unsalted margarine (optional)*

For Serving:

• *Finely ground Parmesan cheddar*

Rules:

1. As per group rules, cook pasta. Set aside 1 cup of pasta water, channel the pasta, and spot it back in the pot.

2. In the meantime, in a sweeping skillet, heat the oil to medium. Add the garlic and cook until it begins to sizzle, for around 1 second.

3. Add chicken, season with red pepper drops and 1/2 teaspoon of salt and pepper, and cook for 4-5 minutes, breaking into little pieces, until almost cooked through. Add the wine and air pocket until for all intents and purposes evaporated, 2 minutes or close.

4. To mix, add stock and toss, and afterward, by then, bring to a stew. Overlay in the lemon punch, flavors, and Parmesan cheddar. Wipe out from heat and at whatever point used, add spread, blend and toss until disintegrated.

5. Toss with rigatoni and 1/2 cup of pasta water held, adding seriously accepting the pasta looks dry. In the event that fundamental, top with additional Parmesa

Citrusy Shrimp-Stuffed Avocados

(Ready in a brief time frame, Serve 4, Difficulty: Easy) Nutrition per Serving: Calories: 420, Proteins: 31 g, Carbohydrates: 13 g, Fat: 29 g, Saturated Fat: 5 g, Sodium: 430 mg, Fiber: 7 g.

Fixings:

• little shallot, finely separated

• ¼ cup of mayonnaise

• tablespoons of harsh cream

• tablespoons of lime juice

• 2 tablespoons of pressed orange

• 453 gramsof separated cooked shelled shrimp

• 1 cup of grape tomatoes, split

• 1 Serrano of Chile, gently cut

* *2 prepared avocados, split, pits killed*

For Garnish:

* *Cilantro*

For Serving:

* *Sweet potato chips*

Rules:

1. Whisk the shallot, mayonnaise, pressed orange, bitter cream, lime juice, and a huge part of a teaspoon of salt in a little bowl.

2. Put the shrimp, onions, bean stew, and a major piece of the dressing in a significant bowl.

3. Spoon in the avocado parts to serve and shower with the overabundance dressing. Improve with cilantro, then, serve for specific chips of sweet potato.

(Ready in a brief time frame, Serve 6, Difficulty: Easy) Nutrition per Serving: Calories: 231, Proteins: 30 g, Carbohydrates: 42 g, Fat: 14 g, Saturated Fat: 2 g, Sodium: 750 mg, Fiber: 5 g.

Fixings:

• *453 grams of skinless, boneless chicken chests, cut into 1" pieces*

• *3 tablespoon of olive oil*

• *½ teaspoon of ground coriander*

• *½ teaspoon of. dried oregano*

• *pot of grape tomatoes*

• *cloves of garlic, separated*

- tablespoons of new lemon juice

- ½ head of romaine lettuce, annihilated

- green onions, pitifully cut

- ½ cup of sliced dill

- 4 pitas, warmed

For Serving:

- Lemon wedges

Rules:

1. Heat grill on medium-high. Toss chicken with one tablespoon of oil, then, fit salt and pepper with coriander, oregano, and 1/4 teaspoon each. Onto the sticks with string.

2. On a tremendous piece of unshakable foil, put the tomatoes and garlic cloves Sprinkle each with 1/4 teaspoon of fit salt and pepper and one tablespoon oil. To shape a pocket, wrinkle and crease the foil.

3. Put pocket and sticks on the grill. Cook for 8-10 minutes, turning the pocket and turning the sticks occasionally until the chicken is cooked. Brush the chicken with one tablespoon of lemon crush not long before disposing of it from the grill.

4. Meanwhile, toss the broccoli, onions, and dill in the bowl with the overabundance of one tablespoon of oil, two tablespoons of lemon juice and 1/4 teaspoon of certified salt and pepper each.

5. Serve pitas and lemon with chicken, tomatoes, and salad.

Steak Chimichurri

(Arranged rapidly, Serve 6, Difficulty: Easy) Nutrition per Serving: Proteins: 0 g, Carbohydrates: 1 g, Fat: 8 g, Cholesterol: 0 mg, Sodium: 15 mg, Sugars: 0 g.

Fixings:

• 16 ounces of mixed youngster peppers

• 3 tablespoon of olive oil, isolated

• 2 12 ounces of strip steaks (around 1 ½ in. thick), made due

• 2 tablespoons of red wine vinegar

• 2 scallions, finely hacked

• little garlic glove, ground

• ½ gigantic red chili(seeded), finely sliced

• ½ cup of sliced level leaf parsley

• ½ cup of hacked cilantro

Bearings:

1. Heat grill to medium. Toss the peppers in a wide bowl with one tablespoon of oil and 1/4 teaspoon of salt and pepper. Season the steak with ½ teaspoon of salt and pepper.

2. Grill steak and peppers, wrapped, some of the time turning peppers until gently consumed and sensitive, 5-7 minutes. Add the steak and cook until required, 5-8 minutes on the different sides. Move the peppers to the bowl and steak to the cutting burden up and leave for somewhere near 5 minutes to rest before cutting.

3. Meanwhile, mix the vinegar, scallions, garlic, stew, and the extra 2 tablespoons of oil in a little bowl and crush all of the salt and pepper. Blend in the parsley and cilantro, add the steak and peppers and serve.

(Arranged rapidly, Serve 6, Difficulty: Easy) Nutrition per serving: Calories: 370, Proteins: 37 g, Carbohydrates: 37 g, Fat: 9 g, Saturated Fat: 4 g, Sodium: 990 mg, Fiber: 10 g.

Fixings:

* *4 cups of riced cauliflower*

* *¼ cup of water*

* *4 skinless, boneless chicken-chest cutlets*

* *2 teaspoon of olive oil*

* *¼ cup of further developed cream of coconut*

* *2 tablespoons of hot sauce*

* *2 limes, split*

• *1(15-ounces) holder of dull beans, flushed and exhausted*

For Garnish:

• *Hacked Cilantro*

Headings:

1. Merge rice cauliflower and water on high for 6 minutes, cover with vented plastic wrap, and microwave.

2. In the meantime, brush the chicken with olive oil and season with 1/2 teaspoon of pepper and salt all over the place. Grill for 5 minutes all around, turning over once almost through. Whisk together the coconut further developed cream and the hot sauce, then, brush on the chicken. Grill until cooked through (165 degrees Fahrenheit), brushing and turning 2 extra times, around 5 minutes longer. Grill 2 limes, isolated, for 2-3 minutes until gently scorched.

3. Toss the dim beans and 1/4 teaspoon of salt with the cooked cauliflower. Serve chicken with limes over cauliflower, enriched with divided cilantro.

1.   Veggie sweetheart Holiday Roast with Mashed Vegetables

(Ready in a brief time frame, Serve 4-6, Difficulty: Easy) Nutrition per Serving: Calories: 246, Proteins: 19 g, Carbohydrates: 22 g, Fat: 9 g, Fiber: 3g.

Fixings:

*   1, 1 lb. (thawed out) veggie sweetheart stuffed cook

*   2 cups diced potato

*   2 cups diced carrots

*   cup diced yellow onion

*   ¾-1 cup of veggie stock

*   4 minced garlic cloves

*   1 tablespoon almond milk

- *1 teaspoon olive oil*

- *Salt and pepper to taste*

Rules:

1. In your strain cooker, heat the oil.

2. Cook the garlic and onion for brief when it is hot.

3. Add the vegetables, salt, and potatoes and join.

4. On top of the vegetables, put the feast on top and flood the stock.

5. Cover the top and seal it

6. Select 'manual' and cook for 8 minutes at low strain or around 6 minutes at high pressure.

7. Hit 'drop' and quick conveyance when the time is up.

8. Let the dinner out.

9. For the vegetables, add almond milk and pepper and smash to your ideal consistency.

10. Serve.

GOOD LIFE!

www.ingramcontent.com/pod-product-compliance
Lightning Source LLC
Chambersburg PA
CBHW060945050726
47592CB00003B/1118